Remembering Lethe

Remembering
LETHE

POEMS BY
Brian Culhane

ABLE MUSE PRESS

Able Muse Press

www.ablemusepress.com

Printed in the United States of America

Library of Congress Cataloging-in-Publication Data

Names: Culhane, Brian, author.
Title: Remembering lethe : poems / Brian Culhane.
Description: San Jose, CA : Able Muse Press, 2021.
Identifiers: LCCN 2020055987 (print) | LCCN 2020055988 (ebook) |
   ISBN 9781773490861 (paperback) | ISBN 9781773490878 (ebook)
Subjects: LCGFT: Poetry.
Classification: LCC PS3553.U2855 R46 2021 (print) | LCC PS3553.U2855
   (ebook) | DDC 811/.54--dc23
LC record available at https://lccn.loc.gov/2020055987
LC ebook record available at https://lccn.loc.gov/2020055988

Cover image: *Combustion* by Tommy Ingberg,
   www.ingberg.com

Cover & book design by Alexander Pepple

Brian Culhane photograph (page 69) by Michael Ito Edmonson

Able Muse Press is an imprint of *Able Muse: A Review of Poetry, Prose & Art*—at
   www.ablemuse.com

Able Muse Press
   467 Saratoga Avenue #602
   San Jose, CA 95129

for Christopher Z. Hobson

Acknowledgments

I am grateful to the editors of the following journals, where these poems originally appeared, sometimes in earlier versions:

Able Muse: "Two Sides of Insomnia" and "Philosopher's Wool"

Blackbird: "The Oxford English Dictionary" and "Imperium: A Bedtime Story"

Chimaera: "On Not Being Able to Name the Seven Wonders of the Ancient World"

The Cincinnati Review: "Just before, or Right after, the Fall of Rome"

Harvard Review Online: "Epitaphs for Epic"

The Hudson Review: "The First Line Was the Last to Be Written"

Literary Imagination: "A Crack in the Amphora"

The Massachusetts Review: "Babel Diary"

Memorious: "Marginalia in Time of War"

Parhelion: "In a Late Hour," "One Day in the Life," and "The Dispossessed"

Parnassus: "The Essay"

Plume: "Remembering Lethe," "A Meeting," "Standing by a Coppice Gate, Reading 'The Darkling Thrush,'" and "Eurydice"

The Raintown Review: "The Accident"

Salamander: "Derivations"

The Sewanee Review: "Alexander in New York, 1979," "*A Large Fine River God Almost Intact* (part two of 'Two Sonnets in Stone')," "The Dante Dictionary," and "Tolstoyan"

Slate: "Declaration to a Shade"

Southwest Review: "The Stoic's Pine" and "Longhand"

"Monody with a Line from Rupert Brooke" appeared in *The Plume Anthology of Poetry 2013*, ed. Daniel Lawless.

"Philosopher's Wool" appeared in *Able Muse Anthology: Best of the First Decade of Poetry, Fiction, Nonfiction, and Art*, ed. Alexander Pepple.

"The Stoic's Pine" and "The Essay" appeared on *Poetry Daily*.

"Just before, or Right after, the Fall of Rome" appeared on *Verse Daily*.

I am especially grateful for summers spent at the Virginia Center for the Creative Arts and at MacDowell, where some of the above poems were first conceived. The Artist Trust of Washington State provided welcome financial support in the form of a writing fellowship. Warm thanks are due to Michael Spence, Robert McNamara, and Hailey Leithauser for their sage suggestions and their friendship.

Contents

vii   Acknowledgments

I

5   After Oblivion

6   The Essay

7   Monody with a Line from Rupert Brooke

8   Longhand

9   The Oxford English Dictionary

10   Derivations

12   The Stoic's Pine

14   Two Sonnets in Stone

16   The Dante Dictionary

18   In a Late Hour

II

21   Tolstoyan

22   A Crack in the Amphora

23   When I Remembered the *Symposium*

24   Just before, or Right after, the Fall of Rome

26 Babel Diary

28 The Dispossessed

30 Imperium: A Bedtime Story

31 Two Sides of Insomnia

III

35 Standing by a Coppice Gate, Reading
    "The Darkling Thrush"

36 Silent Reading

38 Declaration to a Shade

40 Marginalia in Time of War

42 One Day in the Life

44 Alexander in New York, 1979

IV

47 Eurydice

48 Remembering Lethe

52 On Not Being Able to Name
    the Seven Wonders of the Ancient World

54 The Accident

56 A Meeting

57 Etiology

58 Philosopher's Wool

61 Representative Man

62 Epitaphs for Epic

63 The First Line Was the Last to Be Written

65 Notes

Lethe (lee-thee): in Classical Greek, the word (λήθη) literally means oblivion, forgetfulness, or concealment. In mythology, the River Lethe exists in the underworld, where souls who drink its waters lose memory of their former life, thereby allowing for reincarnation.

Remembering Lethe

I

After Oblivion

This is the hour of wind when kneeling
Souls beside the riverbank lose feeling

This the hour of ditchwater on tongue
Swallowing histories of moon and sun

A riverine murmur of muddled thought
Tributary to everything the heart has brought

Then ready to climb the spiraling stair
A stranger once more set free to err

The Essay

for Tom Doelger

I have asked my students once again to write on a theme.
The subject is not the end of the summer,
Though summer has once again ended and they are here.
The subject is not even the coming of autumn

Or the Shakespearean sonnet's use of the couplet.
No, theirs is such a dark and rich theme that their essays
Will look at first like Kafka's diaries—with self-portraits,
Wraiths, and ominous clocks lodged in the margins.

I want each to follow the footsteps of the psychopomp
And find the Gates of Horn where so many have stood before.
Should they be frightened, the pure ether may calm them,
Moving over their hot foreheads with a mother's touch.

I watch them bend low to their work, smudging ink,
Capitalizing proper nouns, stopping only to hurry forward,
Their nibs heavy oars, their scribbling an uneasy rowing.
The dread of conclusions scrunches their shoulders.

One girl wearing her hair up for the very first time
Raises her hand and, at my nod, walks up to my desk.
She has finished first. Her paragraphs have the weight
Of Etruscan tombs, and her face is that same shade of rose

That glimmers in the background of Pompeian frescoes.
I accept that her script is cuneiform and that a grave puzzle
Awaits my midnight's musing. For hers is the lost language
Of the young, a smooth stone I weigh in my palm, and let go.

Monody with a Line from Rupert Brooke

It's only the wind tapping on the pane.
No words, nothing whispered, no news.
They say that the Dead die not, but remain.

Boulevards glisten in freezing rain.
Back and forth, walk ones and twos.
It's only the wind tapping on the pane.

The dog looks up from where she's lain:
A screech crisscrosses slick avenues.
They say that the Dead die not, but remain.

But what can the living hope to gain?
Hear that sound? The scuffle of shoes!
Oh, only the wind tapping on the pane.

Sleet and more sleet: tonight's refrain,
A sound no one willingly would choose.
They say that the Dead die not, but remain.

The dog whimpers over and over again.
No words. Nothing whispered. No news.
They say that the Dead die not, but remain.
It's only the wind tapping on the pane.

Longhand

Here, try it right now. Put pen to unlined paper.
Hold the attention just so, and distantly think of
How under a glass tumbler, magnificently unaware,
Two red ants fought a much larger black foe

On a windowsill where, his journal before him,
Thoreau could observe the battle with magnifying lens,
A half-hour skirmish ending when, its feelers broken,
The larger struggles to rid itself of two severed heads

Still alive, amazingly, fastened to its sides,
"Like ghastly trophies." And he, their ironic god:
"I never learned what party was victorious, nor
The cause of the war." If you copy out that sentence,

Press down on any particular word. Your ink will darken.
Dates are important, even if added retrospectively:
"Observed five years before the passage of Webster's
Fugitive-Slave Act." And, still more distantly, consider,

As you lean on elbow, how the longhand of thought
Always must contend with the world at hand, how
Bruno, threatened with iron pins through lips and tongue,
Would not recant the work his fluent hand had done.

(Hands and work burnt in 1600.) Day by day, struggle
To see clearly. So what if your handwriting's atrocious?
By pressing down harder you'll perhaps cross the abyss
Between words, though no margin of safety's promised us.

The Oxford English Dictionary

While some struggled to return from war,
Others found refuge in pigeonholed words,
Where the occasional surcease in sleuthing
Might open a path with a satisfactory end:

The way Tolkien, laboring in the W's, brought
His vast word-hoard to bear on one *walrus*—
Tusked, blubbery, whale-horse athwart a floe.
In a crabbed hand, he wrote *hrosshvalr*,

Old English source if "zoologically improbable."
Jamieson, keeper of the Skerries Lighthouse,
Contemporaneously reported a beast "yawning
During its sleep" and "quite tolerant of ladies."

Fresh from no-man's-land, the lexicographer
Dug trenches through multitudinous tongues,
Having *walnut* behind him and *warlock* ahead.
And we? *Waterboard. Weaponize.* Worse.

Derivations

As the limestone of the continent consists of infinite masses of the shells of animalcules, so language is made up of images or tropes, which now, in their secondary use, have long ceased to remind us of their poetic origin.

—Ralph Waldo Emerson, "The Poet"

Trivia
There's brisk trade in random facts
At the meeting of three roads:
Each offers what the other lacks,
Murmuring beside wagonloads.

Cell
Robert Hooke, looking down at cork,
Under the first microscope,
Thought of monks praying in the dark
And of their bare rooms lit by hope.

Fiasco
If a glassblower's breaths inspire
Molten glass for seconds too long,
A flaw gathers form in fire:
The glowing cup's completely wrong.

Clue

Each labyrinth contains one clue:
Unwound yarn leading back to light,
Past arches, rooms, stairs, vaults—then through
Doorways, always turning right.

Asterisk

At the end, something like a star
(Whose birth is just an afterthought)
Sends you looking, near and far,
For what you didn't know you sought.*

*Thus, as Emerson once wrote,
All language is a fossil poem:
Found, like some Viking longboat,
With oars still poised beneath the loam.

The Stoic's Pine

for Willard Spiegelman

Persistence has lent this tall white pine
In old age an upstanding vigor, as branch
And bole, though showing telltale patches
Of blight, seem to say, "You too may stanch
Dripping sap or knit broken limbs in time,
If you but accept pain, take joy in snatches."

The white pine's belief in ancient virtue
Stems from one hot serendipitous noon
You took M. Aurelius outside for hours,
Reading on a bed of pine needles; soon
You'd fallen into the just sleep of the True,
And could not see the pine use all its powers

To tap the *Meditations* with siphoning root
Until, by capillary action, it filled its head
With worthy intentions: to stand erect,
To lean neither too far left nor right, to wed
Height to the life of mind and abjure the brute
Charm of wanton grove or willowy sect.

But more: from philosophy it understood how
Ice storms, gnawing beetles, and human young
(Boys' pocket knives probe and torture bark)
Could be faced with solemn, if quite unsung,
Fortitude; how a natural end to every bough
Must come; and how a sharp crack in the dark

Only presages what's already planted in ground
From the start: the quietus life moves toward,
Whether standing still or nodding in the sun.
Had it to face chainsaw and be rendered board,
While another might make a mournful sound,
A soughing in wind, this pine, its last minute begun,

Would recall that serene equipoise and calm
An emperor once praised as the surest sign
Of the settled soul; before the canted snarling cut,
It would tighten inner concentric rings and resign
Itself to hurt, as those who seek the victor's palm
Must pass the Colosseum's gate and hear it shut.

Two Sonnets in Stone

Newly Discovered in the Spyglass

Comes the latest splotch of upthrust letters:
Swart chunks of pumice, shell-studded shale,
Petrified thunderhead's lone black sail,
Rude rim of rock the blunt ocean batters,
Where storm-thronging gulls shudder the long night,
Then darken skies; where breakers throw and throw
Foam on gap-toothed slag as splattered guano
Brindles monolith. Nothing's ever right
Once metamorphosed in cooled corded coils,
Pahoehoe, or set in domino cliffs
Whose scoriaceous slabs quiet our ifs
And buts with promise of pink-reefed corals.
Today's breeze freshens: whitecaps lick round
This volcanic yawp, remnant of spat sound.

A Large Fine River God Almost Intact

Five centuries back, from a pit in Rome,
A large fine river god was slowly raised
Almost intact, but for the beard's clipped stone.
A crowd wondered how time's arrow had grazed
Just that bit, leaving the lithe limbs alone
(One arm coiled to throw a spear), amazed
War and flood dislocated hair, not bone,
And left a slivered fault on which men gazed.
Then Michelangelo said, *Bring me clay!*
And promptly showed how the beard had been worn
Knotted in front.
                No master's touch today.
What have I dredged from the marl? From mind torn,
Nude and broken? It is myself I find—
My sunlit flaw a hairline crack in rhyme.

The Dante Dictionary

I take down my copy of the Dante dictionary
And look up the names of those put in Hell.
I read column after column, turning pages,
Scouring their sins. Each arcane history,

Each infinitesimal internecine feud,
Guelf and Ghibelline, back and forth,
Over sixty-three years. What human drama!
Like that sinner who "gives the figs"

To God, his finger rammed into the hole
Made by opposing thumb and forefinger.
I look him up: Vanni Fucci, whose carcass
Eternally rises phoenix-like from its own ash.

Noosed around his neck a serpent, for he stole,
He admits, from the treasury of San Jacopo;
Unrepentant still, he ignites among the robbers.
Dante says the serpent's sting turns his flesh

Instantly to ash, faster than any *O* or *I*
Was ever written by the hand of man.
And Vanni to him: *To be seen in this state*
By you is worse by far than any death.

What makes it so? Mere embarrassment?
The dictionary does not say. His entry ends
With Vulcan's son, one Cacus, a centaur,
Wildly cantering over to punish him.

I must find out why this crazed centaur
Is also stung to ash by the fangs of snakes,
But that is for another evening's study,
Another myth, another fuming revenant.

It's late, time to close this learned book
With its whiffs of burnt clothing,
Its far-off battle cries, its red-letter dates
So unlike my own view of the afterlife,

Which I picture looking like the Hudson
In November, that stretch on Riverside Drive
Where a lone runner used to pass me at dawn
Without so much as a wave of her hand.

In a Late Hour

In a late hour, thoughts of death—well, yours—
Come with the territory, with the good scotch
Held up to the standing lamp, a golden amber so
Beautiful it begs not to be drunk—well, not begs,
But you understand, don't you, you not there
To raise a glass or offer up a fitting toast,
You who should be in that chair, facing me,
Who would honor you with this raised glass
And tell of fevers dreamt, broken—and you?
Would you look as if to say, Go ahead and drink,
Drink to the living and to the dead, drink to me
And to the memory of who I was, drink peaty
Whiskey and remember my sitting here like this
Listening in the dark, one of us perhaps saying,
"Satie is beautiful this time of day, the *Gnossiennes*,"
Ah the solo piano, yes, so reminiscent of autumn—
"The woods decay," you say in the gloaming,
"The woods decay and fall," and I answer, yes,
"The vapors weep their burthen to the ground,"
And you nod, and drink your drink in my mind,
And smile as though our antiphonal chiming
Struck just the right note, so that when you say,
"I always made an awkward bow," I know it's Keats
Ending his last letter, who just before had written
"I can scarcely bid you good bye, even in a letter,"
But I don't need to tell you that, do I? for you nod
As if speaking to yourself, and swirl your whiskey,
And look at me, even now, even at this late hour,
Long ago borne on a winter wind, your wool coat
Flapping, hat at a jaunty angle, already gone before
I can call out, before the wind slams shut the door.

II

Tolstoyan

for Susan McGrath

This time of year, I always think of winters
Met in Russian novels, the snows on the river
Crossed by a bridge of prose, and someone
Waiting on the far side whose breath spirals
Up into the heavens, whose body leans over
An iron railing, whose spirit is as radiant as ice;
And I am reminded of those long afternoons
Wholly absorbed by aristocratic intrigue—
With carriages and dress balls and mothers
Standing in the wings; how in bemusement
I lovingly partook of my favorites' vexations,
Warming my hands by the fire of their passions.
So I passed the bitter evenings of my youth,
Lost in a world lost to me and to the world.

A Crack in the Amphora

If you can squeeze your eyes through,
Past the dry outer world of painted clay,
You'll find a corridor leading away
From light, away from museum hum,
To the interior a sculptor's palm knew
As wet, before any votive oil splashed in.

Then follow the crack to its dim source:
A star-fracture made millennia back
When a pensive slave wholly lost track
Of his steps, dreaming of his son home
From war, dreaming of his own course
That ill-starred day he'd gone off alone

To gather in his flock before the snows,
Forgetting—as he once more felt the chill
Of seeing crested horsemen on that hill—
To watch a low lintel. Follow his gaze
As he picks himself up and then grows
Pale, seeing a break in the earthen glaze,

A wound soon to be mirrored on skin
When the master's come to claim his own.
The jar's provenance is thereby known
Only to those who journey to the core
Of darkness that lies unbroken within.
Come, touch the cold-pressed dark, and pour.

When I Remembered the *Symposium*

What I remembered is the way Alcibiades bursts in
drunk, reeling around the couches and wine jars,
drunk on his handsomeness and on being flirty,
while the men have been sedately debating eros,
which is why I thought of how Aristophanes half-
seriously told a mythic tale of conjoined doubled
bodies, with limbs turned away from one another,
face averted from face, weird round beings who
spun around doing crazed cartwheels like clowns,
until Zeus—I forget why—finally sunders them,
something the playwright said explains our search
for the missing one whose clasp could make us whole,
which must be how it was I remembered Alcibiades
this afternoon, watching my wife work her garden,
messing around in the dirt in her fluent way of bending
and humming to herself, with lopped-off fleshy bits
tossed every now and then into a yellow plastic bin,
which explains my recollecting the *Symposium*, once
read on a tarpaper rooftop in Tel Aviv above the sea,
thinking what eros meant translated from the Greek,
passion being too shallow, trite, and yet how difficult to
grasp, even double-armed as I am, leaning for minutes
on a sink, wishing I could weave over and whisper
something you alone can translate as eros, a mumbled
breathing in your ear sounding like what Alcibiades
wished to whisper in his teacher Socrates's ear, the two
at night before a battle, when he first knew he loved him,
which is why I recall how beautiful you are in our sixties
as you wipe off the dog's paws with a rag and look up.

Just before, or Right after, the Fall of Rome

for Mary Anne Christy

Lately, I have been thinking again
of the fall of imperial Rome.
Not the fall itself, not that precise moment,
but the preceding hours, even minutes,
of which few reports survive
(recall, it took weeks to break through
the main aqueducts,
axes and picks in rolling shifts),
as well as the minutes
in the immediate aftermath, about which
more's known—though much remains speculation,
a piecing together of wild tales
as out from hemlock forests
legionnaires staggered unhorsed, purblind,
not realizing they had truly lived past
a date every schoolboy knows
or used to know (history not being
what it once was).

Just before or right after,
when a girl could be found still humming in her bath,
a sprig of thyme wilting on a table,
a pile of decrees burnt in the Forum,
the word for surrender mispronounced—

that's what's most alluring:
the hours, minutes, just before and right after
the catastrophe,
when something important,
even life-changing, seems so imminent,
and then not, almost here,
then nearly gone,
like so much of our lives,
the mere seconds before and after
with talk of battering rams, dragonflies, small beer—
worrying endlessly, and then not,
no sooner predicted than lamented,
waiting for some wry Gibbon
to remark on page 753
that such and such killed
so and so, or was killed
by so and so, who then slipped
on the Senate steps
and became a nobody
in the eye of history,
in the eye of the whirlwind
whose Gorgon-pupil opens wide
and admits no wrong.

Babel Diary

What is Kipperman? Describe his trousers.
I go into the mill. What is a mill? Describe.

Two emaciated horses, describe the horses.

Describe the forest.

What are our soldiers?

What is Bolshevism? A Pole?

Aftermath of a pogrom,
A looted Polish estate: a chest of precious books:
Old folios from the time of Nicholas 1
And smashed intimate feminine accessories,
Remnants of butter in a butter dish—newlyweds?

A peasant complains that his horse is swollen
With milk, they took away his foal.

What is Grishchuk? Submissiveness, endless silence,
Boundless indolence. Fifty versts from home,
Hasn't been home in six years, doesn't run.

Describe the air, the soldiers.

Describe the bazaar, baskets of cherries.

Inside of a tavern.
Describe the orderlies—the divisional chief of staff
And the others.

What is this gluttonous, pitiful, tall youth,
With his soft voice, droopy soul, and sharp mind?

Describe this unendurable rain.

Describe the wounded.

The intolerable desire to sleep—describe.

And from Babel's box in the KGB archive,
The arrest in 1939, mug shots, confession.
The expression in profile—glassesless.
One black eye (monocle haematoma).
Seventy-two hours of continuous interrogation.
Admits to spying, sending André Malraux
Secrets of Soviet aviation.

At the twenty-nine minute trial, he recants:
"I accused myself falsely.
I am innocent. I have never been a spy.
I am asking only for one thing—let me finish my work."

The firing squad.
The wall in the basement of the Lubyanka.
The communal grave.

Describe this unendurable rain.

Describe the wounded.

The intolerable desire to sleep—describe.

The Dispossessed

The King and Cordelia ought by no means to have dy'd, and therefore Mr Tate has very justly alter'd that particular, which must disgust the Reader and Audience to have Vertue and Piety meet so unjust a Reward. . . .

—*Charles Gildon on Nahum Tate's expurgated* King Lear

To hear the actor declaim it, to hear those words
In the grip of hurt pride, old father upended,
Spoken coldly, judgment grim, lines the actor
Speaks with finality, with anger and courtly gravity,
Then, turning away from one child's ingratitude,
The King glows with benevolence, for he knows
He is wise and just, his words, his sentence, wise,
And indeed his other daughters nod meekly,
While their estranged sister will find her end
Soon enough in a prison cell—*poor Fool hang'd*—
Curtain ready to come down, but look! she steps
Past entanglements, lightly steps offstage,
Unbowed by pain, while the audience, hushed,
Bent over knees, awaits a further spurt of blood,
As Goneril's poisoned Regan, then killed herself:
Cordelia's murder must be *now*—yet she walks
Boldly right into their midst, radiating health,
Called to life by one Nahum Tate who's blotted
The Fool out of his manuscript, let Cordelia
And Edgar fall in love and a blessedly sane Lear
Retire in peace at the welcome end of Act V,
Ceding to Cordelia his throne, who even now exits,

In all her finery, out onto the streets of London,
Happy that she gets to live out her reign in an era
Where fools can be expunged from nature's mirror,
And where even a Cornwall can resist gall and knife,
Charmed by the discovery that a harmonious family
Is worth more than any butchery, that a blasted oak
On the world's heath need not be a criticism of life,
However much a dramaturge demands love swing
From the rafters, however much we daily watch good
Daughters floating face down in the sea, and fathers
Gripping gunwales, and mothers wailing, maddened—
All the outcast damned floundering in storms, fleeing
Civil war, malice, some helped up by unwilling hands,
Only to linger in a camp's air, in shanties and breadlines,
Under tarps and corrugated tin, behind barbed wire,
Where dispossessed wake the dawn with blank verse cries.

Imperium: A Bedtime Story

In the story of civilization there is this:
Charlemagne conquering Saxons
Made them choose baptism or death.

After beheading 4500 in one day,
He set out for Thionville—the road quite
Wintry, horses awash with bloody snow—
Where he'd celebrate the Lord's nativity.

I tell you this so you will fall asleep
Thinking of the rise and fall of empire,
As the tabby buries her nose in wool
And squints contentedly.
                          For Hegel,
The spirit of philosophy would rule
In some future age. *Geist* he called it.
Armies still ride along that muddy road.

Lullaby: beat, beat of horse hooves.

The Venerable Bede dictated
To the boy scribe Wilberht
Right up to the hour of his death,
His voice breaking against
The wet hills of Northumbria.
His only worldly goods, "a few treasures,"
In a box he ordered brought to him,
So he could hand them out, at the last—
Some pepper, napkins, incense.

Now close your eyes.

Two Sides of Insomnia

1
My old dog had an idea and almost rose,
Then thought better of it—thus the night goes.

Sleeplessness turns upon itself like prose
A bored translator only halfway knows.

Now overhead those undertaker crows
Caw caw as a black wind grows.

Forty, fifty. The decades, body blows.
Night staggers on. A hall lamp glows.

2
Reaching the point of no return:
To slide from warm bed,
Bent over as if trying to relearn
The way downstairs, as ahead

The night extends, the gray streets
Less familiar than before.
Listen: wind buffets wave, repeats,
Up and down the shore.

III

Standing by a Coppice Gate, Reading "The Darkling Thrush"

1899—century's grave. A city gate loomed,
Left ajar, while one blast-beruffled thrush
Sang to December's bine-stems. Poor bird.

I pictured it, pitied it. Much later I learned
Coppice was not another word for copper,
Nor *bine* evergreen exactly. A fire burned

Through mists: meanings shape-shifted
Until the dictionary won out and the gate
Led to a *thicket,* bine to a *twining plant.*

Nevertheless, Hardy's aged thrush remains
More pigeon than thrush—with a dash of sparrow—
And just as beautiful as its wind-rushed name.

Nothing can wholly unlearn past ignorance,
And I may never tell apart thrush's note
(Cold, wet, darkling, midnight's, London's)

From the lark's at heaven's gate. So I read on,
Half right, half wrong. Again, I feel a boy's joy
That is two parts darkness, one part song.

Silent Reading

Nietzsche proclaimed our ears quite dead:
The modern reader clenches tongue
And reads with voice inside his head
What ought to be directly wrung

From vocal cords as public sound
And shouted to the ceiling fan
Or shyly stammered on damp ground.
In antiquity, reading man

Spoke to anyone around, brought
To glissading diphthongs a bright
Intonation, to daring thought
Added his voice's oversight.

Augustine confessed himself struck
By the strange habit of Ambrose
Who, given half a chance, would duck
Into a vestibule with prose

He never muttered, the pages
Turning without companion tone:
His silence in saintly stages
Making him more and more alone.

So, we lie in bed together,
If apart, eyes perusing books:
You lost in some dirty weather,
While your heroine stumbles, looks

At her lover, and breaks things off—
While I interrogate a play
Whose main character gives a cough
When greeting one he must betray.

Glancing over to you, I read
A sentence from your chapter's end.
You barely hear a hum. Thus freed,
I take up my own coughing friend

And speak aloud his last best speech.
You tilt your head as if to say
Something slightly beyond my reach,
But truly nothing about the play,

Or what the silenced years have cost,
Or why I read that part to you.
We turned to what we thought we'd lost,
As from deep reading you withdrew

To better grasp my utter sense.
If, thereafter, hearing grew weak,
Our passion's perfect present tense
Gave tongue to what we needn't speak.

Declaration to a Shade

In 1397, Carlo I Malatesta defeated Mantua and
ordered the statue of Virgil destroyed; in 1936, Hitler
ordered Mendelssohn's statue in Leipzig destroyed.

What little I have to declare I do so,
Before the statue of Mendelssohn tipped over,
Before the statue of Virgil also tipped over
For whatever reason proffered—racial laws,
The enmity of the victors for the losers, etc.—
What little baggage I have I now hand over
To the ministers in the Ministry
Gazing down on the snowy public square,
Its toppled statuary and bewildered pigeons.
Surely the weather *is* miserable, they say.
Still, kindergarteners lark about in parks
As hatless mothers chat in the market stalls,
As denounced painters, composers, poets
Dream of a sudden reprieve from on high.
Instead, always the walk to the guillotine:
They paint the sky with broken fingers,
Hymning sunlight to a pocketful of fleas.
What little I have to declare I do so,
What little knowledge of their sorrows
I have, what little of their trials I know:
Such I shall bear beyond any ring of fire,
Where the tomb of the unknowns is found
In the spoor of a fox, huddle of brackish ferns,
Purgatorial plumage of ash-gray storks;
Where, according to local legend, the lame

Muster along a gritty ditch, still muttering
About the things that used to matter most—
And should one surface to take my arm,
I'll step down and cross the marish waste
And turn toward the brittle winter wind,
Offering this least resplendent of tributes,
Breathing the musk of desecrated names.

Marginalia in Time of War

On the side of this sheet
(No use looking)
Or on the back
(No use)
Stand stiffened figures

Women
Those who fell at the fall of Berlin '45
To Russian officers foul if suave
To proles victorious drunk roaring
(No use)

Sisters cousins mothers grandmothers
Yes and the very young
Taken (no)
Sometimes three or four times
In the night after night

Nothing helped of course
Except to become an officer's special prize
(Briseis
Helen
You too knew that)

Some faked illness
Under sheets in a typhus ward
Or hid in attics like others before them
Anywhere a closet trunk crawlspace grandfather clock
Stifling breaths

On the back of this paper
Or at the ragged margin
To the left
Or at the straight-ruled right
Holding on

Here is plunder
A slim-limbed Berliner gazing
She stands at this rickety window
On the far side of war
Looking out

One Day in the Life

for Michael Ito Edmonson

It was the winter I taught Solzhenitsyn to young people
Who wrote due dates on colorful calendars, who
Moodily drew geometrical proofs, conjugated *to be*
In various languages, and ate lunch while I would watch
Snow fall on the Quad, snow that did not in any way
Resemble the snow Ivan Denisovich stood stiffly in,
At attention, waiting for his squad to be let into camp,
The men standing in either summer or winter boots
(They had to choose only a single pair on arrival), all
This in a landmass called Siberia, which my students
Had looked up on the first day of our discussion.
"Solzhenitsyn wrote his book in 1962, fifty years ago,"
I tell them. And they say, "The story's boring." And I say,
"But what does it say about the human spirit? and what
Does it say about the need for storytelling? Even there,
Even as they starve or get sent to the isolation cells,
The prisoners nonetheless crave stories about home:
Two girls met in a railway carriage, an afternoon swim
On an estate's pond, a huge carp caught after great battle,
A father forgiving his errant son who had gone off
Until the one evening when he returned, but too late."

"Well," a boy answers, leaning back in his chair, "the book
Isn't a page turner and it was practically impossible
To keep eyes open and that's why I didn't do the reading,
But I'll make it up by reading twice as much tonight."
"No," another says, "I don't think the book's so boring.

It wasn't exciting, but it was interesting how they worked
Harder than they had to, building that wall, how work
Gave men some pride." We talked about the masonry,
And then the period was over before I could tell them
Solzhenitsyn was himself imprisoned for a letter
Making fun of Stalin, how he watched through his bars
The fireworks marking the end of the world war, how
He and the other prisoners, having nothing to celebrate,
Looked on as all Moscow cheered. Or that his was a time
When a joke could mean eight years in a work camp.

Perhaps Shakespearean tragedy's more foreign than purges,
The divine right of kings more baffling than mass murder,
Yet as I prepare the questions for their exam tomorrow,
I consider: What yarns do we tell ourselves to escape
The slag heaps of the present, as a new century unfurls?
How will future readers view our own attempts at justice,
Our same compulsions to philosophize, our same
Sorry excuses? Milosz writes of old age,
                              That it befell others,
This I can understand, but why me?
                              But why *me*, why
Must I, creature of uncertain worth, get up each morning,
Blinking and grayer, to find myself no closer to knowledge
Than I was when Solzhenitsyn first published his *Day*?
How is it that we've plumbed black holes and dark matter,
And yet the crudest human motive resists scrutiny,
As we hunker down over a weak flame to tell our tales?
That each new decade advances another ramrod dictator,
As we write our songs of defiance and loss, as we stand
In the snow, swaying in felt boots, counting the days?

Alexander in New York, 1979

The professor of Greek, prematurely frail,
Chain-smoked while describing a halting circuit
Around the room, her cane beating out ahead,
As she rhapsodized about her favorite period,
For in it, she declared, we could recognize
The lineaments of our own age. Young, naive,
We thought she meant Macedonians in Asia Minor
Had been young, naive.

                        Take Alexander, she said.
Alexander burned with a flame sparked by whom?
The answer: Aristotle, who had been Plato's pupil.
We too were pupils! Whom would we spark?
This thought was lost in her story of Alexander's
Skeleton becoming a bathetic source of infighting
After the boy-general's death. At that she stopped,
Tapping ferrule against a withered leg. But why?
What caused Ptolemy to squabble over bones?
We did not know. Perhaps an obscure funerary rite,
Offered a hesitant soul. Not so! Supernaturalism:
He who held his bones held the mortal coil's power.
Symbolic transference right out of *The Golden Bough*.

We nodded. Beyond, the city rose mild and beautiful.
Spring had come early. We were young and brilliant,
Undismayed by all the stories we had yet to learn.
Our beauty would never end in a scuffle over bones.
On twin adamantine towers, suns would ever burn.

IV

Eurydice

Their legend is a look in the eyes of the one
Who stops and must look back. That one.
We name him and we name her, in the story
Handed down—whose details always blur.
There's something so appalling in his need.
The terrible desire to turn, if just once,
To see if the beloved comes. Making certain,
Just once, that those slurred footsteps are hers.

There's something so natural in his look back.
It reminds me of how, in turning to gaze
At a maple blazing with reds last October,
My eyes lost it in the split-second after,
As I turned back to the curving road ahead,
The present like a cold wheel in my hands.

Remembering Lethe

Yesterday, a friend wrote:
So many of your poems are about
Ancient facts, names. I don't know
Those references, but nonetheless
I think what you do admirable.

Not to be understood *is* admirable
If seen in a certain light: a way
Of keeping up one's old allusions.
Hardly what my teenage self
Had sought to wrap mind around

During lectures on the Greek nude
When slides taught me to embrace
New embodiments of grace and see
Why, expressionless and wooden,
The Kritios Boy is beautiful.

How was I to know that those
Deep images from my school days
Would be so crucial decades on?
How, before I'd ever climbed
Delphi's crags, a vision of Delphi

Was to capture me so wholly
I could almost taste the fumes
That wound from the sacred fissure
At whose lip the priestess knelt
To suck in the upwelling god.

My son once asked the name
Of that river in Hades said
To make the newly dead lose
Memory. Lethe? Lethe, I think.
In her last year, my mother

Gazed at me and saw no son
But her former husband—*James,
Come up here*! She motioned
To the bed she lay on, and I
Answered with a stricken *No.*

No, she said, *I want you up here!*
I do not know why the scene
Fades: an unbridgeable gulf.
And what did we do afterwards?
Probably a wheelchair outing

To the Home's garden where
She smiled at roses with the look
Of one who had known names
For this, this. . . . Sinking into sleep.
Did she understand she'd stay

In that place? Or how finally
A phone would waken her sons
With wished-for, dreaded news
Leading to a dawn flight toward
Frayed robes, unworn slippers?

Well, we would all be better for
A dip in Lethe water to ward off
The cold when the cold comes.
In a file, I've kept my son's crayon
Drawing of the souls gathered

By the riverside, their ferryman
Just a brown scribble bobbing
Next to stick figures on the bank,
Ready for their mythic entrance
In some long-ago show-and-tell.

If I touch her absence now it's in
Stories I almost hear as falling asleep
I dream a riverbed's weeds thrust
And catch at the hem of memory,
A cloak unraveling, unspooled.

Here, mother, take my hand again
The way you used to on our way
To wherever we were headed, when
I would look up at you wordlessly
In tongue-tied love. And you? You

Were so young, too, and childhoods
We shared, mine in your keeping,
And yours as we settled on the bed,
Your warming voice joining years
When I was just your age making us

Almost playmates together, though
Finally you would have to stand up
To reenter your world—leaving me
On the riverbank, child no more,
Seeing your shadow cross into light.

On Not Being Able to Name the Seven
Wonders of the Ancient World

I can recall the musty encyclopedia turned
To that article, darkening on the yellowed page,
And I can summon, if the room is quiet,
The black and white rendering of the Pharos,
Whose reconstructed light magically burned
Once more, if only in a boy's eyes—a stage
Of adolescence when supernal facts lit
The candle of learning, and through the house

I swayed to the drumbeat of storied names,
As Latin, Sumerian, Saxon, and Greek
Pierced the manifest dullness of my life:
Hercules's Labors and the Seven Wonders,
Hierarchies of angels and bracketed reigns
Of pagan kings. I studied, book to cheek,
Index finger tracing mythologies' strife
Past pyramid, tower, dolmen; thunder's

Flash the shaking of Zeus's aegis or Titan
Battling old Chronos; persimmon's seeds
The hardened tears of Demeter's grief.
Job's plagues could actually be counted,
And counted they would miraculously lighten
My numberless burdens—all trivial deeds
From the outer world of sun, rock, and leaf,
Which, in comparison, hardly amounted

To anything at all, although somehow
That gallery of commonplace hours
Has lately come to mind—snowball fights
In Central Park and a friend's sudden fist;
Dawn's walk, head down, to school—as now
The Hanging Garden's incandescent showers
Fade to a picture of those wide-eyed nights
When wonders I used to know could fill a list.

The Accident

Strolling once again in a deserted terminal,
You pause before the newsstand's headline
Of the latest crash, and far back in your mind
You hear, from months ago, a sharp whine
Of engines churning and the tremor of a final
Swoon: how you saw the future then unwind

In scant seconds—a none-too-subtle warning
To review transgressions in the cabin window's
Cold plastic pane. All your sins stretched out
Just as readable as a coastline in the morning:
The red and white roofs in haphazard rows,
And no one walking down below to give a shout

Of recognition. But the wings wobbled level
And reality regained its casual hum; the captain
Took the intercom with a chuckle and said
North Atlantic winds could get a mite bit evil,
Not to worry. Indeed, the awful whirring din
Suddenly went internal: a throbbing in your head.

Now today's news with its foreboding of shocks
Still to be delivered, heralded by a tightening throat:
An elevator that hurtles down a dead-end shaft;
A train overshooting a trestle; a taut pleasure boat,
Upside down in a gale, missing promised life raft.
Who knows when your body will founder on rocks?

Or, will you breathe easier because of an accident
That ramifies well beyond the minute you lost
Your car keys and had to take a much later plane?
Then, too, consider the absolute (if unknown) cost
Of reading this to the very last line: shall you gain
Years thereby, or miss more than you ever meant?

A Meeting

Of all the disappointments
Consider those great men
Who passed each other smoking cigars
In some hotel corridor
Looking each for his own key,
Like Joyce and Proust meeting once,
Just once!
And Joyce so tired he fell asleep at their dinner.
Think of that opportunity,
The amazing glittering remarks
On the novel's mimesis of time.
Or take the afternoon I met Kenneth Burke
Through his son-in-law, who wrangled me an invitation
(To a farm in New Jersey, I recall).
I carried, fresh from grad school,
A copy of *Grammar of Motives*
The stooped, tousle-haired philosopher inscribed,
Which I have since lost.
Nor can I remember a single thing he said.
Once, in my father's last illness,
We spent a whole week alone together.
Each day I sponged and fed him,
And took his sugar count.
All that time he did not say a word,
Even when I'd come with the needle.
I believe he probably knew I was there—
I'm positive he did for one moment,
Our eyes meeting over the wreckage of his chest.
Then he moved his head, gravely,
As if just looking away to clear his thoughts,
Only to turn to the wall.

Etiology

I showed him my shaking shaking hand
And the doctor, a specialist in shaking,
Shook his head, No, which I believed
Meant perhaps, No, don't worry, or, yes,
Even better, No, don't be silly, or taking
My hand in his two palms, No, it's fine,
Normal, see them every day, don't trouble
Yourself, I've seen worse, oh far worse.
But instead he looked longingly at me
And touched his lips to my right hand,
Or seemed to, his eyes so close to skin,
Eyelashes brushing my crinkled lifeline,
And shrugged saying, No, I don't know
What you are shaking about, could it be
The news, how the boors have won out
In the Capitol? Or something overheard
On the train, something about whether
Or not earthlings will populate galaxies?
The cost of wheat? A quake, leagues off,
Which may even now be sending a tsunami
To overwhelm us all? No, putting down
My hand and gazing out the office window,
You are merely the victim of some prank
Whose cure lies far beyond my skill to mend,
Though I take this stethoscope to your chest
And listen to your blood beat in my ears
And tell you not to worry, you may one day
Live in a house in a village and raise a garden,
The flowers of which will rise and fall with
The seasons, and you may find peace there,
When knowledge comes calling at the last.

Philosopher's Wool

Eager alchemists
Shaking stubborn fists
At the universe
Often made things worse
For those standing by
Whose astonished cry
Could be heard through walls
As black smoke filled halls:
Is this truly wise?
What if someone dies?!
An unholy blast
Might expunge the past
When flame touched cow's blood,
Saltpeter and mud,
Or burned base metal
In an old kettle
Until the whole room
Stank of common doom,
Of unwashed sinners
(Mere rank beginners)
Stumbling ahead
With incautious tread
On the littered floor
Where, amid the gore,
Truth was said to lie
Waiting for some dye
To imbue with gold
(As writers of old
Had said would happen)

Ordinary men.
Surely, it was thought,
Wealth was what art brought
To occult research.
From Minerva's perch
The owl flies aslant,
Though we think it can't,
And must hit the mark
Even in the dark.
So in alchemy
The learned set free
In a certain flame
What is zinc by name
("Philosopher's wool"
In an ancient school),
As such metal learns
Flight by what it burns
And drizzles down white
If the timing's right.

A history of zinc
Hardly makes us think,
Except by way of
Likenesses to love,
Which, when heated, too
Becomes something new
As it changes shape
Under magic's cape.
Once zinc turns to snow,
Its flight up may show
Heights lovers will fall

Should they, after all,
Succumb to that state—
A precipitate,
An alloy of pain,
A chalky gray stain,
Which whitens with flakes
What it most mistakes
To be kindred hate.
Interanimate,
Love and hate obey,
Through this very day,
Laws that come from high;
Centuries go by
And still we hope and fail,
Still mix the pail
Of our desire,
Still look in fire
For crucible's gold,
Though we cannot hold
Nature to account
If gold becomes zinc
As the missing link
Is thus missed again
In a dirty rain.
Zinc is wool, we're told.
So let love be gold,
Elusive at best
Or a kind of test
Whose secret's best kept
When salt rain is wept.

Representative Man

Iron-hearted man-slaying Achilles
    —W. H. Auden, "The Shield of Achilles"

The weak-of-knee fought
To avoid Achilles's fate:
The two-pronged epithet
Reserved for the first-rate.

Better to hunker down,
An anonymous pawn,
Than blunder boldly in
The rosy-fingered dawn.

Epitaphs for Epic

Aeneas shouldered his father and then took
   Troy with him in a final backward look.

Byzantium enchanted William Yeats
   As civil war tore down ancestral gates.

Penelope raveled and raveled thread
   Before repairing to her marriage bed.

Armor bravely worn without condign skill:
   Myrmidons mourned before they paused to kill.

Rather some farmer *up there* than *here* a god—
   Or so Achilles gestured under sod.

The First Line Was the Last to Be Written

The first line was the last to be written,
Ash in the fireplace first to be stirred;
Apples in the bowl last to be bitten,
Waters in the mountains first to be heard.

The first line was the last to be written,
Frost lay white on the wintering herd;
The first wool made the last child's mitten,
The last pen wrote *the purring cat purred.*

On the open page the last word written,
Next to the lamp the opening word;
Last season's apples yet to be bitten,
Far from the tumult first to be heard.

The last page was the first to be written,
Waters in the mountains O very cold;
Ash in the fireplace, wool under kitten,
On the open page the last word is told.

The first line was the last to be given,
Ash in the fireplace first to be stirred;
Peace in the capital last to be riven,
On the open page the purring cat purred.

"Monody with a Line from Rupert Brooke" on page 7: See Brooke's "Clouds."

"Derivations" on page 10: The etymology of "fiasco" is uncertain, but John Ciardi, in *The Borrower's Dictionary*, traces it to the term for an irreversible mistake made by Italian glassblowers. "Clue" derives from *clew*, "a ball of thread or yarn . . . originally in reference to the clew of thread given by Ariadne to Theseus to use as a guide out of the Labyrinth. . . . The purely figurative sense of 'that which points the way,' without regard to labyrinths, is from 1620s" (*Online Etymology Dictionary*).

"Two Sonnets in Stone" on page 14: Both the title, *"A Large Fine River God Almost Intact,"* and the story of Michelangelo's reconstruction of the god's beard can be found in Castelvetro's *Commentary on Aristotle's* Poetics.

"The Dante Dictionary" on page 16: The figure "sixty-three years" refers to the duration of the struggle between Guelfs and Ghibellines in Florence, as given in Toynbee's *A Dictionary of Proper Names and Notable Matters in the Works of Dante*, itself the dictionary of the poem's title.

"Babel Diary" on page 26: A found poem derived from fragments of Isaac Babel's diary and KGB records, reordered and slightly edited from those cited in Elif Batuman's *The Possessed: Adventures with Russian Books and the People Who Read Them.*

"The Dispossessed" on page 28: Gildon, "Remarks on the Plays of Shakespeare" (1710): Tate revised *King Lear* in 1681 so that audiences would not be put off by the original's constituent tragedies; Tate's version, wherein poetic justice prevails, became the standard for the stage for over 150 years.

"Standing by a Coppice Gate, Reading 'The Darkling Thrush'" on page 35: "century's graveyard": Originally titled "By the Century's Deathbed, 1900," "The Darkling Thrush" was first published in December of that year.

"Silent Reading" on page 36: James Fenton (in "Read My Lips," *The Guardian*) cites Nietzsche's censure of modern readers: "The German does not read aloud, does not read for the ear, but merely with his eyes: he has put his ears away in the drawer" (*Beyond Good and Evil*). Alberto Manguel claims Augustine's description of Ambrose's silent reading marks "the first definite instance [of the practice] recorded in Western literature" (*A History of Reading*).

"Marginalia in Time of War" on page 40: Certain details are drawn from *A Woman in Berlin: Eight Weeks in the Conquered City—A Diary* by Anonymous.

"Philosopher's Wool" on page 58: From *Wikipedia*'s "Zinc" entry: "Some alchemists called [burned zinc] *lana philosophica*, Latin for 'philosopher's wool,' because it collected in wooly tufts, while others thought it looked like white snow and named it *nix album*."

Brian Culhane's *The King's Question* (Graywolf Press, 2008) won the Poetry Foundation's Emily Dickinson Award for a first book by an author over fifty. His poems have appeared widely in such journals as the *Hudson Review,* the *New Criterion*, the *New Republic*, and the *Paris Review*. After getting his MFA at Columbia University, he received a PhD in English  literature from the University of Washington, where he focused on epic literature and the history of criticism. The recipient of fellowships from Washington State's Artist Trust, MacDowell, and the Virginia Center for the Creative Arts, he now divides his time between New York's Catskills and Seattle.

Also from Able Muse Press

Jacob M. Appel, *The Cynic in Extremis: Poems*

William Baer, *Times Square and Other Stories; New Jersey Noir: A Novel; New Jersey Noir (Cape May): A Novel; New Jersey Noir (Barnegat Light): A Novel*

Lee Harlin Bahan, *A Year of Mourning (Petrarch): Translation*

Melissa Balmain, *Walking in on People (Able Muse Book Award for Poetry)*

Ben Berman, *Strange Borderlands: Poems; Figuring in the Figure: Poems*

David Berman, *Progressions of the Mind: Poems*

Lorna Knowles Blake, *Green Hill (Able Muse Book Award for Poetry)*

Michael Cantor, *Life in the Second Circle: Poems*

Catherine Chandler, *Lines of Flight: Poems*

William Conelly, *Uncontested Grounds: Poems*

Maryann Corbett, *Credo for the Checkout Line in Winter: Poems; Street View: Poems; In Code: Poems*

Will Cordeiro, *Trap Street (Able Muse Book Award for Poetry)*

Brian Culhane, *Remembering Lethe: Poems*

John Philip Drury, *Sea Level Rising: Poems*

Rhina P. Espaillat, *And After All: Poems*

Anna M. Evans, *Under Dark Waters: Surviving the Titanic: Poems*

Stephen Gibson, *Frida Kahlo in Fort Lauderdale: Poems*

D. R. Goodman, *Greed: A Confession: Poems*

Carrie Green, *Studies of Familiar Birds: Poems*

Margaret Ann Griffiths, *Grasshopper: The Poetry of M A Griffiths*

Janis Harrington, *How to Cut a Woman in Half: Poems*

Katie Hartsock, *Bed of Impatiens: Poems*

Elise Hempel, *Second Rain: Poems*

Jan D. Hodge, *Taking Shape: Carmina figurata; The Bard & Scheherazade Keep Company: Poems*

Ellen Kaufman, *House Music: Poems; Double-Parked, with Tosca: Poems*

Len Krisak, *Say What You Will (Able Muse Book Award for Poetry)*

Emily Leithauser, *The Borrowed World (Able Muse Book Award for Poetry)*

Hailey Leithauser, *Saint Worm: Poems*

Carol Light, *Heaven from Steam: Poems*

Kate Light, *Character Shoes: Poems*

April Lindner, *This Bed Our Bodies Shaped: Poems*

Martin McGovern, *Bad Fame: Poems*

Jeredith Merrin, *Cup: Poems*

Richard Moore, *Selected Poems;*
   The Rule That Liberates: An Expanded Edition: Selected Essays

Richard Newman, *All the Wasted Beauty of the World: Poems*

Alfred Nicol, *Animal Psalms: Poems*

Deirdre O'Connor, *The Cupped Field (Able Muse Book Award for Poetry)*

Frank Osen, *Virtue, Big as Sin (Able Muse Book Award for Poetry)*

Alexander Pepple (Editor), *Able Muse Anthology;*
   Able Muse: A Review of Poetry, Prose & Art (semiannual, winter 2010 on)

James Pollock, *Sailing to Babylon: Poems*

Aaron Poochigian, *The Cosmic Purr: Poems; Manhattanite*
   (Able Muse Book Award for Poetry)

Tatiana Forero Puerta, *Cleaning the Ghost Room: Poems*

Jennifer Reeser, *Indigenous: Poems; Strong Feather: Poems*

John Ridland, *Sir Gawain and the Green Knight (Anonymous): Translation;*
   Pearl (Anonymous): Translation

Stephen Scaer, *Pumpkin Chucking: Poems*

Hollis Seamon, *Corporeality: Stories*

Ed Shacklee, *The Blind Loon: A Bestiary*

Carrie Shipers, *Cause for Concern (Able Muse Book Award for Poetry)*

Matthew Buckley Smith, *Dirge for an Imaginary World*
   (Able Muse Book Award for Poetry)

Susan de Sola, *Frozen Charlotte: Poems*

Barbara Ellen Sorensen, *Compositions of the Dead Playing Flutes: Poems*

Rebecca Starks, *Time Is Always Now: Poems; Fetch, Muse: Poems*

Sally Thomas, *Motherland: Poems*

Paulette Demers Turco (Editor), *The Powow River Poets Anthology II*

Rosemerry Wahtola Trommer, *Naked for Tea: Poems*

Wendy Videlock, *Slingshots and Love Plums: Poems;*
   The Dark Gnu and Other Poems; Nevertheless: Poems

Richard Wakefield, *A Vertical Mile: Poems; Terminal Park: Poems*

Gail White, *Asperity Street: Poems*

Chelsea Woodard, *Vellum: Poems*

Rob Wright, *Last Wishes: Poems*

CPSIA information can be obtained
at www.ICGtesting.com
Printed in the USA
FSHW010106170921
84821FS